Life of a *Difference*

DR. HEDRINE M. NANA

ISBN: 978-0-578-68304-1

Publishing production: Dr. Patricia Ross, HugoHousePublishers.com

Cover and Interior Layout : Ronda Taylor, HeartworkPublishing.com

Contents

Preface

*L*ife of a Difference is a collection of spirit-filled poems that illustrate the power of salvation. The purpose is to invoke the inner mind on the understanding of the mighty power of God, the power of salvation, the unconditional love of God, and the emptiness of life. The poems will uplift your spirit and help you in your journey as you accept Jesus Christ as your Lord and Savior. These poems will also renew or reaffirm your commitment to our Lord Jesus Christ if you have accepted him into your life.

The writing of the poems was solely inspired by the power of the Holy Spirit who equipped me with His power and enabled me to write all of the poems within one month. My writing of the poems is a spiritual gift that emanate from God. In the beginning, He gave me two poems in two separate dreams titled, "The Intention of a Friend," and "You Are a Friend." When I woke up, I vividly remember the title of the two poems, and then I knew within me it was time to start writing to glorify God.

Since I love to write, my readiness allowed the spirit of God to manifest within me. It was like the words were downloaded to me, complete in stanzas and in expression. I felt like the poems were already written, and God used me as a transcriber to bring them to reality. As children of God, we should understand life as solely dependent on God. We are His vessel to do His will, for He is our creator. *Life of a Difference* creates a magnetic connection with God that fills your heart with His love and enables you to live a life pleasing to Him as you avail life in totality for Him.

As you read the poems, it will open your mind and feed your Spirit with the magnificent love of God. The poems highlight the importance of gaining salvation that brings new beginnings for the mighty work for God. These powerful poems will enrich you with the knowledge of God by giving you a clear understanding of the power of God within you. I pray that you will be transformed with the poetry as I have and find a renewed life in the spirit of

God. Life will always create new beginnings full of surprises, and no matter where you are on your spiritual journey, may you find a new life in Christ Jesus.

Acknowledgments and Dedication

This book came to reality by the manifestation of the power of the Holy Spirit. All glory belongs to Almighty God who has empowered and enriched me with knowledge and wisdom.

This book is dedicated to my husband, Sammy Tchana Nana, and my six beautiful children—Dorcas, Samantha-Maxine, Kyle, Nobert, Ezra, and Alexander-Samuel Nana.

To my mother, Bertha Iyabie Misodi and my belated father, Nobert Chukwuemeka Ohiakwu, thank you for bringing me into this world, fulfilling the will of God.

My special love to my grandmother, the late Mrs. Racheal IyaTua Besumbu, for her selflessness and caring. Thank you for nurturing me to be the woman I am today.

Also, thank you my spiritual mother, Evangelist Belema Abili, with Princess Belenzy Ministries, for your spitiual guidance and teachings and fulfilling your assignment for my salvation.

A Life of a Difference

I did not know the life of a difference
I was lost in the world.
I was living in blindness and ignorance,
For I knew no difference.

I know His name, but did not know Him
I know He exists, but know little of His existence.
I was lost in the world,
For I knew no difference.

I was busy of the things of life,
striving to satisfy myself and my desires
knowing life as gaining fame, possession, and power
For I knew no difference

I was in a dream land
Where everyone knows no difference.
A land of blindness, ignorance, and selfishness
A land of hatred, jealousy, unforgiveness, lavishness, and pride
I woke up from this dream, and now I know the difference.

I can see clearer and everything is brighter with the light
I know the difference, for the light makes a difference.
In the light you can see what others cannot see
You can do what others cannot do
For you know the difference.

You can walk without stumbling,
For the light makes a great difference.
A life without the light is no life
But a life with the light makes a difference.

Now I can see for everything is brighter and clearer
A life of difference is a life of salvation.
No one can see what I see for I dwell in the light.
For I know the difference

A life of difference is a life of fulfillment
I know the difference for the light dwells in me.
A life of difference is a life of salvation.
Now I am different, for I know the difference

Your Love for Me

Your love for me is unconditional and endless,
For you are love.
Your love is limitless, boundless, and overflowing.
Your love is ageless and new every morning.

You love me more than a father loves his son,
And nothing can ever separate me from our love.
You love me even before my creation
Your love never changes.

As a river constantly flows, so does your love for me.
When everything cease to be, your love continues to exist.
Your love is unexplainable, indescribably
Exquisite and astounding.

Your love for me
Is incomparable, unmeasurable, and uncountable,
For you are love.
Your love never judges and finds no fault.

On the mountain top and in the valley low
Your love is assurable.
Your love is everlasting.
Everyday your love is poured over me

Like a morning dew that rejuvenates.
How did I deserve your love?
Because you love me, life is worth living
Teach me how to love you as you love me.

The Power Within Me

If only you can imagine this mighty power
You will be amazed at His mighty strength.
If only you can imagine His powerful ability
You will be amazed at His marvelous function.

If only you can imagine His wonderful capability
You will be amazed at His swift mission.
If only you can imagine His hours of operation
You will be amazed that He never slumbers.

If only you can imagine Him as a person
You will be amazed at His friendship.
If only you can imagine Him as the greatest scholar
You will be amazed how much you will learn.

If only you can imagine His attentiveness
You will be amazed that He constantly speaks.
If only you can imagine His mission for you
You will value His presence every moment.

He is the mighty power within you
The power that is always active. It never sleeps.

The Holy Spirit

His name speaks for himself, for He is holy
His habitation is purity and holiness.
He who seeks Him in wholeness finds Him,
For He never forces Himself on anyone. He is gentle and meek.

He reveals Himself to those who seek Him in genuineness.
He dwells in those who accept Him.
He is in communion with those who acknowledge Him
and communicates with those who listen to Him.

He teaches those who understands Him.
He shows up for those who depend on Him.
He loves to communicate with you
And loves to communion with you.

He loves you to rely on Him
and loves you to please Him.
He is a helper when you need Him
His utmost mission is to lead you to righteousness

He is a person
         he is a friend,
                  he is a Holy Spirit
He is gentle, meek, and pure.

         He is the spirit of God.

The Encounter

Wait for the appointed time
When your mind and soul is in unity
When your heart is pure and knows no evil
When it is repentant of wrongdoing
And is receptive to newness.

For it is time for your encounter with God.
When the encounter comes unexpectedly
No one can recount the sequence
No one can dictate the occurrence
Or decide the event.

It is time for your encounter with God.
The encounter is a powerful experience
No one can recount.
The encounter is a fascinating experience
No one can dictate.

The encounter is a glorious experience
No one can explain.
The encounter is the powerful manifestation
Of God's power and love for His children.

The encounter is the beginning of a new journey
A journey for accomplishments.
The encounter is the beginning of life
A life of potential and fulfillment of destiny.

The encounter brings a life of transformation
A life of restoration, new inspiration, and empowerment.
Wait for the appointed time,
For it will come when you desire God.

Wait for the appointed time,
For it will come when your ways please God.
Desire to receive the Encounter, and you shall be filled.
Wait for the appointed time.
That time is here, for it is the Holy Ghost encounter.

My Life Without You

My life without you is a lonely life
        a wasteful life
        a life of sorrow.
My life without you is a worthless life.

You give me joy when I am in misery
You bring me hope when I am hopeless
You comfort me when I am weary
You nourish me when I am hungry.

You clothe me when I am naked.
You protect me when I am in danger
You give me happiness when sorrow abounds
You are close to me when I am abandoned.

I cannot live without you,
For you are all I have.
My life without you
Is a life of despair and anguish.

I cannot live without you,
For you make me whole.
You teach me all things
That I need to know about life.

I cannot imagine my life without you
For you are a true friend.

The Presence of God

The presence of God is within me
I can feel it
For His glory manifests in His children.

The presence of God is around me
I can sense it
For His glory surrounds His children.

The presence of God is above me
I can touch it
For His glory crowns His children.

The presence of God is everywhere
I can see it
For His creation evinces His glory.

I can feel it
       sense it
              touch it
I can see it everywhere.

For the presence of God
Is within me, around me, and above me
It is everywhere.

You Are a Friend

You are a friend. I call you my friend
Friendship is revealed by action.
I call you my friend
For friendship stands the test of time.

We are created to bond together
As life reveals itself to us.
We are created to cherish one another
As life carries us along.

We are created to stand for one another
As life's troubles resolve themselves.
We are created to forgive one another
As life gives allowance to one's fault.

We are created to love one another
As life is built on love.
We are created to celebrate one another
As life gives its goodness.

You are my friend, for you bond with me.
       you cherish me
       you stand by me
       you forgive me.

You are my friend, for you celebrate me.
You are my friend, for you love me genuinely.

The Mystery of God

Who can tell about the majestic being?
No one can fathom His origination.
Who can tell about His habitation?
No one can envision His majestic throne.

Who can tell about His mighty thought?
No one can perceive His mysterious plans.
Who can stand before His radiant throne?
No one is pure enough to compare to His holiness.

Who can narrate His ways of creation?
No one can describe His marvelous works.
Who can tell about His intention?
No one can imagine His wondrous compassion.

Who can withstand His majestic power?
No one can confront His glorious throne.
Everyone is powerless before Him,
For he existed before creation.

He is the creator, yet no one has ever seen Him
No one can tell of His being, mind, plans, and intention
Except His spirit reveals them to you.
He is pure, He is holy, He is a magnificent king.

Only if you know the mystery of His existence
Will you reverence his holiness and purity.
Only if you can see the radiance of His glory
Will you depend on His mighty power.

Only if you know His intention for you
Will you glorify His holy name.
We are His children and His intention is good
His throne is in heaven, and He reigns on the earth
He is God by Himself.

Life is a Mirror

Life is a mirror that reflects oneself
      a true reflection of creation
      a true reality of humanity
Life is a mirror that unveils the innermost

Life is a mirror that reflects exactness
      that discloses uniqueness
      that conceals no blemishes
      that self-examines character
Life is a mirror that reveals emotions.

A mirror cannot alter
      nor refute
      nor amend its reflection
For it is a true reflection of perfection or imperfection
A mirror is life as it is.

A mirror is your true self
      It can reflect your works
      It can remind you of your inner being
A mirror reveals emotions that emerge after self-reflection.

Look in the mirror, you have no power to amend your reflection
      and live a life reflective of your true self
Look at the mirror and see life as totally dependent of God
Look at the mirror and see the life that reflects yourself.

A Multi-dimensional God

A mighty power! A mighty God!
He performs manifold wonders
He manifests limitless miracles.

A mighty power, a mighty God.
He rescues promptly in adversity
He functions in precision.
He examines every path one takes

He is ever present
Regardless of the time, place, and situation.
He is on time and active in diverse locations at the same time
He is a multi-dimensional God.

The Intention of a Friend

It is for a good intention
That our friendship abounds.
I invite you to know me
And to learn about our friendship.

When you learn about me as your friend
Then you will know my intention for you.
When you engage your time with me
Then you will understand our companionship.

I am here to help you
When you need me most.
I am here to carry you along
As life's journey sojourns.

I am here to relieve your burden
As you surrender them to me.
I am here to give you peace
When the stress of life brings unhappiness.

I am here to care for you
When all hope is gone.
I am here to bring you happiness and joy—
I am here to be with you as you need me to be.

I Am Not Part of This World

I live in a a world perverted by evil
A world ravaged by sin.
Innocence is plunged into evildoers
And purity transformed into immorality

I can see beyond this world;
I can see beyond my environment
An environment perverted by evil.
I can see beyond my suffering
Suffering amidst the beauty that lies ahead.

I understand life as a journey
A journey that will end unexpectedly.
I live in this world, a world ravaged by sin
I choose to live life as it is, a life of reverence

As I transcend from this evil world
I choose to live life as it is
With admiration of the beautiful creations
And appreciation of existence.

Satisfaction of life's provision
Demonstration of love for one another
Realization of the emptiness of life
I can see beyond this world.

I understand life as a journey
A journey that will end soon.
I live in this world
A world where sin is inescapable.

I chose to live a life as it is, a life of humility
As I transcend from this world
I chose to detach myself
From the things of the world.

I chose to focus on the life beyond,
For the life beyond this world is a life of perfection,
A life of magnificent abundance and peace,
A life of no suffering or turmoil.
I understands life as a journey, a journey to be at home.

God of Precision

He is a God of precision—
The God who never fails in his words or plans

His plans are accurate and perfect
established according to His will for you

He determines your life as a roadmap of who you are
He knows the creation before the conception

He knits you together to a life of perfection
He knows every detail of your life

He takes pleasure in your wellbeing
His words and promises are fulfilled in due time

He is a timely God—
He creates a perfection to fulfill His will for you

He is a God of precision—
He does what pleases Him.

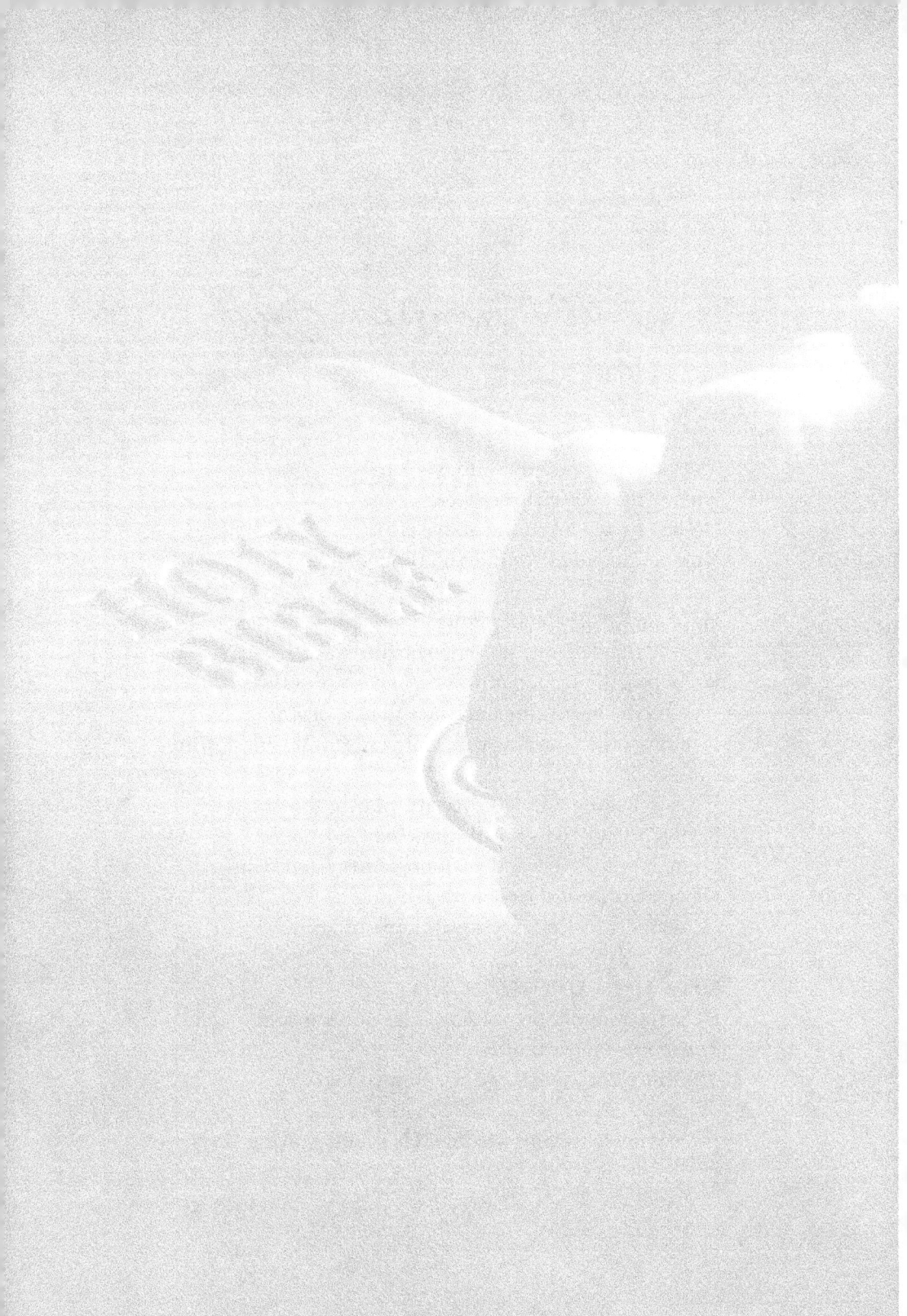

All-Knowing God

The God of knowledge and wisdom
No one hides in His presence
No one knows anything above Him
No one can tell His mind and thoughts.

He knows every detail of our lives
     the past, the present, the future
He knows the second, minutes, and hour of time
     the beginning and the end of everything
He knows the plans for you, a plan to fulfill your destiny.

He is in heaven and His eyes are all over the world
Seek Him, for He is an all-knowing God.
Human knowledge and wisdom comes from Him.
He created the universe with His might.
He delights for you is to know more of Him.

You are created to learn of Him.
He is the foundation of knowledge and wisdom.
The more you learn of Him
The more knowledge and wisdom you receive.

He is knowledge and wisdom. He is all-knowing God.

You Are Not Alone

You are not alone for a mighty power lives in you.
When you feel lonely or abandoned,
Envision this mighty person by you
      For He dwells in you.

At all times He stays with you.
His closeness and his oneness
Cannot be separated or differentiated
      Involve Him in all you do.

Speak to Him, and He will respond.
Ask what you need, and He will provide
Allow Him to lead you in all you do
      Seek His approval, and you will never go wrong

His active engagement is your reverence and holiness.
He is your watchman and shield.
Don't feel lonely or abandoned
      Find solace in his presence

Acknowledge His presence
      For you are not alone.
The Mighty One dwells in you.

Worship

I am created to worship
Before the sunrise until dawn
With bent knees and open arms
As I bow my head with a joyful heart.

I delight in the self-gratification of your presence
Where my mind, soul, and spirit is one
To soak in your holy presence
With no distraction or selfish motives.

I humble myself before you
In your presence I worship in wholeness.
This sweet aroma is your delight to make your day
And brings the heavenly hosts amidst.

For this is where I long to be
For I am created to worship you.
In the midst of worries and tribulations
With a joyful heart I pour my heart.

With a truthful heart and every breath
Where mind, soul, and spirit are one.
All I desire is to worship you,
For I am created to worship you.

The heavenly hosts are with me
This is where I choose to live.
In your presence all day
Where mind, soul, and spirit are one.

To declare your glory is all I want to do
For I am created to worship you.
As I connect to be where you are,
You are the sole occupant of my heart.

You gives me direct connection to you
To rejoice with the heavenly hosts
I want to be where you are
To worship you in wholeness.

I see your smiles and laughter
As the sweet aroma of worship
Embraces your holy face, and
Shocks the earth with your peace.

Your joy brings heavenly showers,
To fulfill my heart's desires.
For all I wish to do
Is to worship you in truth and in spirit.

The Heavenly Realm

I see the lights, bright as white
While a colorful medium of light waves
Travel in a uniform sequence
Across the peaceful atmosphere.

I see the bright day, bright as the sun
Where time is standing still,
A place tranquil and serene
With a variety of colorful vegetation
Swaying in the rhythm of worship.

I see the golden mansion, spacious as home
Sparkling with the reflection of colorful lights
Echoing with a soothing, seamless
Unison of voices that gives me inner peace
And transcends across the glorious worship.

I see countless numbers of ageless beings
Adorned with long white robes
That sweep the radiant floor,
Bowing and singing praises,
Worshipping at the glorious throne.

I see the majestic throne
With glittering gold and lights
So bright to see the Magnificent
Sitting on His majestic throne.

I feel an atmosphere of peace
No sorrow or worries exist
An atmosphere of everlasting joy
A place of perfect home
A home for eternity.

The Finish Line

Life is a race, a race to finish
With an outline for the start and end
Readiness for the finish line
A race of heavenly focus.

Life is a race, a race with a focus
Focus with direction to complete
Equipped for adversity
Challenges that inhibit motion.

Life is a race, a race with a vision
Vision to stay to the finish line
Clear vision without distraction
Compete for the prize.

Life is a race, a race with a set time
Champion is not for the swift
Attitude and attentiveness
Determines the final outcome.

Life is a race, a race with rules
No deviation of the path
Out of focus is out of place
And out of place, is out of the race.

Life is a race, a race to end well
In jubiliation and with completion.
Hardwork deserves a reward
Recognition with a crown.

The Breath of Life

Just like the still water evaporates
Just like the fire smoke disappears
Just like the morning fog disperses

Just like the winter snow melts
Just like the autumn leave decomposes
Just like the evening sun fades

Just like the spring rose withers
Just like the hourglass dissipates
Just like the riverbank washes

Just like the colorful rainbow fades
So does the breath of life vanish in due time
No matter who we are or what we own.

Taking the last breath
A time no one can predict
The time is inescapeable and undiscriminate.
Everyone is equal in the eyes of the Creator.
Though the body is breathless
And every work of life terminates

The soul remains alive
To reunion with his maker for everlasting life.

About the Author

DR. HEDRINE M. NANA was born in Cameroon, West Africa, into a Christian family. At age two, her parents relocated to Umuoma Uli, Anambra State in Eastern Nigeria where Dr. Nana stayed until she was twelve. She moved back to Cameroon to live with her grandmother, a mid-wife in Kumba General Hospital. Living with her grandmother greatly inspired Dr. Nana. She graduated from the University of Yaoundé with a degree in English Language in 1999.

In early 2000, she worked as the Translation Secretary for the Nigerian Embassy Defense Consulate. In August 2001, she immigrated to the United State of America to live with her husband. As soon as she landed, she embarked on her Nursing education, culminating in a Doctorate in Nursing Practice from the University of Texas, Arlington, in 2017. As a nurse practitioner, Dr. Nana has worked with urgent and emergency medicine and is also an associate clinical professor with the University of Texas, Arlington.

Dr. Nana gained salvation in Christ Jesus in February 2017, and her life was totally transformed. She is married and blessed with six beautiful children. She resides with her family in Grand Prairie, Texas.

If you are interested in having Dr. Nana come speak to your congregation, please contact her at spiritfilledpublishing@gmail.com, or you can call her at (469) 628-4247. Dr. Nana speaks about growing up in Africa and how her spiritual encounters have changed her life.